Rules of Su

Ian Harker

Templar Poetry

Published in 2017 by Templar Poetry

Fenelon House
Kingsbridge Terrace
58 Dale Road, Matlock, Derbyshire
DE4 3NB

www.templarpoetry.com

ISBN 978-1-911132-20-2

A CIP catalogue record of this book is available from the British Library

Cover Design and Artwork by Templar Design

Typeset by Pliny

Printed in England

Acknowledgements

I owe a huge thank you to everyone who's read my work and given me feedback, but especially Tom Weir, and the other Hulmans (Andrew Lambeth, Tom Kelly, Suzanne McCardle, Rose Journeaux, Andy Armitage and Anna Sutcliffe). I'm hugely grateful to David Tait, Mary Noonan, Kim Moore and David Borrott for the long-distance critiquing. Thank you to Alex McMillan, who told me what I needed to know rather than what I wanted to hear. And thank you to the Leeds Writers Circle – I owe you all more than I can say.

'Blue God', 'May 2015', 'Thomas Piketty Picks his Way through the Shattered Shopfronts', 'Saatchi Says', 'Urban Legend: Astronauts', 'The Moon is Slanting Over the Rooftops', 'Goldfinches Gatecrash the Arnolfini Wedding', 'The Caretaker Compares Himself to the Happiest Man Alive' and 'Lazarus Awake' appeared in the pamphlet *The End of the Sky* (Templar 2015).

'Thomas Picketty…' was written as part of Helen Mort's Leads to Leeds project.

'Right Now' featured on Carole Bromley's YorkMix poetry blog.

'Saturday Night on the Death Strip' appeared on the New Boots and Pantisocracies blog.

'Aire' was joint winner (poetry category) in the Remembering Oluwale prize, and appeared in the anthology of the same name from Valley Press. Remembering Oluwale won a Saboteur Award in 2017 for Best Anthology.

'Goldfinches Gatecrash the Arnolfini Wedding' appeared in iOTA, issue 95.

Author Photo: Mark Dolby Photography.

for Chris

CONTENTS

POD

The harbour was thick with whales
and dad is hacking into them
with the knife that belonged to his father,
the knife he has a name for. The whales pop and sigh
and he is covered in blood. The waves are black with it.
Dad can hardly breathe. It's like he's been running.
I feel like I'm turning into smoke. "Son," he says,
"Son," and his big hand wipes three red lines across my face.

BIG BLUE

It arrives on the back of a lorry —
surname and signature and it's all yours,
thirty stone of whale heart sitting on the drive.

How big is it? Golf buggy.
Is it true you could swim through the aorta?
Cold around skin around cavity
that's depth charge and cabin pressure,
a noise like blood in your ears.

You are full-length inside it,
barely conscious for all its bellwether.
And inside of you there are all these other hearts,
one inside the other. How many can you hold
in the palm of your hand? Your own heart
about the size of a fist.

FLOOD

My childhood's been flooded out.
Dad wades down the drive with the dog
in his arms, mum helps Mrs Winn with her case,

we were going to stay at grandma's but her house is the same
and my school's almost submerged, a tip of slate sticking out
above a slow-motion playground.

The Crem's gone, too — granddad's coffin sways
down the aisle, the men's black coats swirl like ink,
wreaths bob around our heads.

From Cabbage Hill I can see the divers falling towards us
through the sky, torchlight strafing the silted privet,
the hulls of lifeboats turning back, giving us up.

At the hospital we can hear the weight at the windows.
We stand around her bed and wait for the water
to fill our ears. I hold dad's hand. My breath.

BLUE GOD

That first summer other boys
were tight shadows,
static at the tips of my fingers
till out of a steel-white sky
that could have been cold to the touch
came you – blue like Krishna.

No one else knew.
No one could see the cobalt stream
from under your shirt. I was hot
in a school jumper but my eyes,
closed like a corpse's, opened
and found you – dancing
if you did but know it
at the end of the sky,
at all the far reaches.

And everywhere around you abundance –
petals and filigree, water
through dry earth.
And a point of light under your hand
where all the other light started.

ON WAY

November and it's dark
before you leave King's Cross,
sidings slipping past, connecting trains
held up as people heave themselves
into seats. I see you swaying
through two hundred miles of hedges
and business parks, legs folded in,
your face in two panes of light.

I say text me at Emley Moor.
When my phone goes you'll be forty minutes,
adjacent to the string of red and it's like it was
when I was a kid — Elland Road
was a long roar and my grandma took me
to the window in the back bedroom
and pointed and said that's where your dad is.

And mum in Sheffield for the snooker —
a pile of faces at the Crucible
but I never saw her. There's something
about distance and strangers in glass
and a voice all that way away,
time and distance and the difference
between us and all that light.

MY LOVER USED TO BE
AN OLYMPIC ATHLETE

He said I could hardly stand for the glare
sweat pouring down the line of my spine
the dark smear of my armpits
the ends of my hair

I want to know how it felt —
medal tape thick as four years around his neck
Vitruvian man half naked under the lights

And was he barefoot under the weight
of his own body?
The palms of his hands
the thickening V of his thighs

Could he feel the weight
of the others behind him? Phantom pains
on the parallel bars of his arms

He says blood was swimming in his ears
and he was blind like it was midday

he says it's like a two-way mirror
where you're watching your every move

he says there's a moment in freefall
where you weigh the same as your own shadow

ORPHEUS BY TWOC-LIGHT

Someone lifts the tape and you step over
into the white tent on the towpath, a lightbox
containing what's left of Orpheus the smalltime dealer,
Orpheus the kickboxer they cut up and chucked
into the canal, shit-heap of arms and legs, froth
of blood and spunk, slot machine jackpot clattering
over the weir. Here he is now singing over the sirens,
a car alarm over the junctions and flyovers
and there's the tattoos — the stiff piston of his right arm,
hand cupping his lifeline between forefinger and thumb.
In the flashbulb flashback starry women are tipping sweat
over the pair of you, your body is a twisted sheet around
and underneath him and his mouth is a hole
in the thick of it, brickwide and not like you remember.
You reach down and brush the hair out of his eyes,
white arms exchanging swabs and markers and lenses.
And Orpheus goes on singing into the floodlight.

LIFE DRAWING

There was this apple as high as the ceiling.
It had lines coming off in all directions
and no one could get round it.

Someone took a chainsaw to it
and a man was sitting in the middle.
They tried to draw the pips rolling down his face
like tears, the bruises on his green skin.

When someone bit into his thigh
there was a snapping sound.
The hair on his arms was all leaves.

Most of them drew him at daybreak, a kickboxer
surrounded by windfalls, sketched blossom behind his ears,
a branch between his legs.

SHADOW

The thing that frightens you the most
is that I might get up and walk away,
break off from whatever it is you are doing.

But that isn't how it works.
I can only make you out
from the corner of my eye –
the crease of your arms,
the head to foot of you
getting longer by the minute.

But even in the dark
I lie under you and that's
when we're closest. An arm
reaching out. The shape of you breathing.

RIGHT NOW

alright mate
and I can tell the sender
is head to foot in gantry light,
his profile is a dual carriageway
and when he sends dickpics
the full length of his body is stretched out
in oncoming traffic

not bad fella u?

I want to ask him
if this is how it's going to be
from now on, white light shining
from the palms of our hands

yes m8 u discreet?

I say there's no way
anyone can ever know about this
your screenshot eyes
the swipe right of your smile
your fistful of inches
surrounded by radius

lol.Work 2moro u?

I tell him everything I say
comes out as voicemail
but you've never heard me speak

I say you're getting further away
just by staying still

Location received
Are you sure you want to block this guy?

Where he's sitting
it's always 3AM —
last seen 10 hours ago
his voice white noise
in the long stammer
of the First New Message

MAY 2015

People are going to work.
The stock market has rallied.
It looks like it's going to rain
over the patios and dormers,
the grey pavements and the red-brown rooftops.
It looks like it's going to tip it down
on Scafell Pike and the National Arboretum,
on the Mall and the M1 and the open boats
shoved off into the sea-lanes of the Mediterranean.

And here we all are, frightened eyes
looking over the edge of a cliff,
fingernails white with hanging on.
They can see us from the ships
in the Strait of Dover, a whole country
hanging on for dear life beneath the cry
of gulls, waiting for the boots to come
and crush our hands, begging them
to do it to her, do it to him,
do it to anyone. A whole country.

ZERO HOURS

The thing about our galaxy is
that when you're out beyond the exosphere —
three hundred miles and counting —
the starlight, dead or otherwise, is a solid mass
and there's no stopping it.

You could be forgiven for thinking
that England is a join-the-dots of mountain ranges
and brown signs, three hundred and sixty degrees
of doubleclick around a World Heritage Site.

But the pickers are up all night,
crawling across a whole field on their hands and knees.
Men in high vis are waiting for a minibus
long before the streetlights bang off.

RULES OF SURVIVAL

04:39 your sunrise time
you find yourself among the lines
of business village birches,
the dedicated meeting rooms
and the radial routes,
the grey choke of layby unleaded.

Kicking your heels on the hard shoulder –
one part UK Border to three parts Strait of Dover –
the orbital towns are right behind you
as the sun comes up over the passing places
of the Areas of Outstanding Natural Beauty.
There's never been more rolling news
but all you can think about are the rules of survival:
three minutes without air
three days without water
three weeks without food

LIMA TANGO

Do you know the Lima tango?
Will you dance with me
among the peeling plasterwork
of the year? It is 1933.
Will you sway your way
out of one epoch and into another.

All my brothers are dead.
Sometimes I dream I am a nurse
and I am closing their eyes
one by one, the thump of the guns
never far away, like a heartbeat
on the end of a stethoscope.

But no one closed their eyes.
That's why I won't have children —
I won't bring children into a world
where they might die with no one
to close their eyes. So dance with me.
We haven't got long. On the cusp
of Christ knows what.
Let's dance the Lima tango.

BARLEYCORN

Spring was the worst —
sway and crack of the green pouring back
and he's all ears, away crowd in the hedges,
lungs coming out in foxgloves.

Sun and moon weren't the half of it —
growing pains, fistfuls of dawn chorus,
there were acres and hectares of him tight
against the greenbelt, frantic with the fires of autumn.

And then there was his face:
GM and bee's wing flushed with the longest day,
half blind with hayfever,
twelve hours barefoot in the long lanes.

In winter he was a pisshead
coming home from the pub,
beer-sweat in the midday half-dark,
ditch with a backbone of ice.

Or he was a silo charging off
into the middle distance without another word,
stubborn can't-live-without-him
as far as the eye can see.

Cut in half, there's a man inside
peddling for all he's worth, more armfuls
than he knows what to do with.
"Nature's a forced clock," he says

and you look down to see your bones threshed
into bundles, your body is stretched out
like open fields and as it starts to rain
you can feel yourself taking root.

SATURDAY NIGHT ON THE DEATH STRIP

Imagine what it feels like
to take your shoes and socks off
in the middle of Berlin,
sand between your toes a stone's throw
from Karl-Marx-Allee. Imagine beach huts
in the centre of Berlin near a bend in the river
and realising that where you're sitting
used to be the Death Strip, rat run
between the two walls raked with sand
so that people's footprints showed up
under the searchlights from bricked-up window
to bricked-up window.
How far away are you from Peter Fechter –
eighteen and bleeding to death just out of reach,
you can hear his voice getting fainter with the bleeding
but he's just out of reach, you can hear him shouting
but you're in the line of fire.

These days the Wall is brass marks
in the pavement, runners for a sliding door
people keep forgetting was there
in spite of all the selfies.
We keep forgetting what it was like.
Have you ever knocked a wall through
and felt the whole house change?
How things used to be and whatever it was
you were afraid of. Have you ever noticed the bullet holes
in the Brandenburg Gate? You can't see it from Google Earth,
but the streets of Berlin are covered in names.

STREET VIEW

I know it blindfold –
the fall through the air
and the fade to black,
arrows on the road and the lurch
past cars and lamp-posts,
sky stitched together from different days.

One minute tarmac is drying
from one of those showers that comes
from nowhere. Then the window is open
and sunshine catches something
in the room behind.

I'm waiting for the update:
the lawn torn up,
For Sale sign flapping
from the lilac, lavender bending
under the weight of the bees
then vanishing in a single click.

THOMAS PIKETTY PICKS HIS WAY
THROUGH THE SHATTERED SHOPFRONTS

He's at a conference in Leeds
when the fighting starts.
As soon as he hears he skips the plenary
and heads for the Headrow, the Headrow aglow
with burning riot vans.

Down Briggate the plate glass tinkles
under his feet like small change,
like worthless currency. In the distance
the rattle of small-arms fire,
the tap-tap, tap-tap of Chinooks.

The mannequins eye him as he goes,
arms and legs at all angles,
their high cheekbones,
their catwalk scowls all there is
to suggest their surprise that here,
among the teargas and riot gear,
here outside the chapel of Our Lady
of Teargas is Thomas Piketty,
Piketty who saw through it all,
Piketty who followed the money,
Piketty who saw it coming.

In Harvey Nicks they are lighting candles
at the altar of Our Lady of Teargas,
they are lighting candles for her children
on the streets of Athens and London,
New Orleans and Ferguson, Missouri.
Be with us now in Trafalgar and Tiananmen,
on the Champs Élysées and in Times Square,

be with us as we face the tanks and the truncheons,
the teargas and sirens, your blue
the blue of flashing lights,
the blue of the baton charge.

Piketty steps through the shattered shopfront
into the remains of the foodhall.
The makeshift congregation turns
at the crunch of the glass under his heels.
The celebrant smiles. "You are just in time,"
she says, "to read us the first lesson."

THE SERIAL KILLER IN POPULAR CULTURE

Suddenly the crime scene is a snowglobe
and finding her feet above it is Myra Hindley –
old flame, blown fuse above the house
they're demolishing around her.

For all the witness statements and background noise
she's a burning waxwork – black rings under her eyes,
peroxide fizz caving in and the whole street's out to see it,
the moonlit shriek, the brief midday of her burning up.

All eyes are on the dropped rocket of her body.
Then there's silence before it all goes quiet again.

CARE

Four AM. The children from the Beckett Home
are standing in sepia in the fields
around the ringroad, black and white
except for a blue balloon, each one
holding a blue balloon on a piece of string.

One by one the streetlights flick off
and the balloons lose their grip on gravity,
the children lift gently at arm's length
into the air, each one finding a thermal stair
until the dandelion clock of kids blows
into the daybreak, into the wide blue yonder,
a clutch of blue balloons and patent leather shoes
swinging out of sight into the sunrise.

SCAN

With the brain as blossoming lobes,
higher instincts thinned down to cockpit
or a bullet and accounting for chandeliers
and the music of Beethoven.

And in turn the thickening Rorschach mass
built up by everyone who ever lived —
ground zero at the base of the spine,
a lift shaft strung with fairy lights.

I read an interview with a brain surgeon
where he said every move he made
was a cut through memory itself —
sight, speech, whatever matters is easily destroyed.

And what will survive is not necessarily love
but the proof of it. Before you try to think
how you could prove that love
has been a part of your life,

let me assure you
that you already have.
And what constitutes proof
is far less than you ever imagined.

AIRE

in memory of David Oluwale

Eastgate

There's a change in pressure where a building used to be —
memory of brick and windows, a spot you come across
like dowsing where there wasn't any rain.

They're demolishing Millgarth.
A few years ago David stared it down
from a billboard on the side of the Playhouse
and the hair stood up on the back of my neck.

The Dark Arches

Everything smells of water.
You can't shout for the water,
you come out smelling of water —
it panned down off the hills and came to this,
water slapping the back of your throat,
the weave of the river against the canal,
boxing clever, fighting shy.

The Calls

Friday night in a white teeshirt, straight from work.
You won't believe how cold it is.
The silt comes from nowhere
and you're punchdrunk,
water like a windscreen,
your shoes are downstream with kicking,
you're another pair of shoulders.

New Briggate

Doorway after doorway.
Leave your mark in cardboard,
the sag of it, the cold of the plateglass.
Everyone wants you here – finger and thumb.
If you won't cooperate, if you won't even try.
The footsteps say show willing:
doorway – shopfront – finger and thumb.

Killingbeck

Where water meets earth,
a grave filling like a stairwell.
The dead are the mirror of the living,
all lit up – the living full length,
the dead lying back, grabbing
at their shadows. Millgarth goes down
in a swirl of brickdust – cell doors, white tiles,
time servers walking on thin air.
The lights go out. A grave fills with water.

SAATCHI SAYS

Friday afternoon at the Tate Modern
on the day before the new exhibition
and Charles Saatchi has come on foot
across the Millennium Bridge from the church
of St Magnus Martyr where he has made votive offerings
to Our Lady of Shrieking Madness – Charles Saatchi is here
to supervise the hanging of the new work.

He homes in on a large canvas in the corner
where the artist herself is fretting about the light
swinging by on the drifting logs of the Thames.
"Up a bit," he barks and the man with the cherry picker
brings the canvas up a bit. "Down a bit," Saatchi decides
and in the silence the cherry picker whirrs
the painting down a bit.

"Turn it around," Saatchi says. By this time
the Assistant Director has appeared at Saatchi's elbow
and she asks him what does he mean exactly.
"I mean around," he clarifies and the painting is duly swung
round so that the back is facing out, gaffer tape,
felt tip, an address. "There," Saatchi says. "That's better."

DOUBLE CLICK

One morning you wake up to your streetview self
moving about downstairs, making you breakfast,
smiling on the other side of your scratch-card face.

His shadow is flapping the wrong way, every movement
is a left click and there's nothing to say you aren't trapped here
where Buckingham Palace or the flat where you lost your virginity

are stitched together from different days –
arrows on the road both point the same way to a jumpcut
of sunshine, starter homes rise up around you from the hedgerows.

Why are you seesawing backwards and forwards
in front of the house you grew up in?
Don't you know what time it is? What are you doing here?

URBAN LEGEND: ASTRONAUTS

They say it sends you crazy —
a range of hills at your back,
the ground ahead not much more
than an ellipse and you're staring back
at everything you've ever known.

And what you thought was black
when you stood in the yard staring up
at the tailfins of meteors
or the appendix scar of Hale-Bopp
or the moon that's now inches
from the soles of your feet
is in fact a solid wall of starshine
reflecting in the goldfish glass of your helmet
and you feel like you felt learning to swim
when your mom took her arms away
and the human mind is very very small.

THE MOON IS SLANTING
OVER THE ROOFTOPS

Sylvia Plath said the moon is bald
and wild and maybe it is in Heptonstall
or wherever she was thinking of
but right now it's anything but –
white light is pouring over the wet
black slates like the time I saw a film crew
at the abandoned mill – six months later
it looked dark and grim but that night
from the top deck of the number 42
the fake corpse surrounded by cameramen
smoking and drinking instant coffee
looked like the boot prints and litter
and scrap metal people leave in laybys
and on the north face of Everest
and the light side of the moon
before the latest Apollo kicks itself out
of the fish-tank silt
with an imperceptible thump.

GOLDFINCHES GATECRASH
THE ARNOLFINI WEDDING

The Arnolfinis are concentrating on looking demure,
eyes downward, surrounded by the wealth
that has unloaded itself like bales of wool,
stacks of hay, wealth like tickertape,
wealth like the tick-tick of small stones
in a moleskin bag hanging by a paunchy side
from a Moroccan leather belt.

The Arnolfinis are concentrating on being embarrassed
by the riches – chandeliers, mirrors, small dogs –
when the goldfinches arrive one by one in a line
on the telephone wires outside the window.

The dog goes mad and Mr Arnolfini stiffens
at the noise of the dog and the noise
of the goldfinches and Mrs Arnolfini thinks
he's going to lose his temper again.
"Don't move!" barks Mr van Eyck, but it's too late,
Mr Arnolfini's best hat is skew-whiff, the dog
is scratching at the door to get out
and Mrs Arnolfini – already four months gone –
has given up and let go of her husband's hand and flaked out
on the bed, her dress hitched up over her bump.

Mr Arnolfini yanks the cord of the Venetian blind
and sticks his head out of the window.
The goldfinches are in good form – a handful of gold coins
flung into the street, a line of red dinner plates
looking at Mr Arnolfini quizzically as he flaps his arms
through the casement, shooing them away
like the beggars waiting for him

outside Ladbroke Grove tube station
as he stalks towards the City to forklift
crates of gold bullion into the Thames.

Mr Arnolfini is startled by the gold and black and red
thronging his head, his hatless head.
"You have to come and see this!" he shouts to his wife
who is adjusting her headdress in the mirror.
"Come and look at this, you'll miss it!" Mr Arnolfini is grinning
like a trader at close of play, black and gold and red
flapping around his head. "Come and look at the goldfinches!"

LOVESONG OF A LONELY
PYLON SPOTTER

Sometimes I imagine I'm a pylon
star-jumping my way across the greenbelt,
thousands of volts at the tips of my fingers,
china vertebrae fizzing in the drizzle.

To stand so still with the wind blowing through me!
The inscrutable machinations of sheep at my feet,
my ankles ringed with barbed wire, my brothers and sisters
striding off along the rush and pour of contour.
Pylons sing to each other. Pylons are the puppeteers
that make the country jump and dance.
Pylons are the little men staking the giant
to the ground in his sleep.

You should never miss the chance to get up close
to a pylon, feel its wisdom like standing stones.
Touch one and you are lifting the whole country
with the palm of your hand.

FINISTERRE

That night I knew he'd never be happy.
Everything was still and I asked him
why he missed the sea. He said
it has a clean white smell,
he said when he walks on land
there's still sea under his feet
and when he lies awake his ears
are two shells and when he talks
there's still salt in his voice.
He told me the sky fell in love with the sea
just like he did so when it rains
the sky is crying to be near it,
he told me the sky stretches on
but it will never reach the sea
no matter how hard it tries.

ONLY IF I CAN BE NORWAY

In the orange light of a burning autumn
you turn to me on the back step
and ask if you can be my Sweden –
Sweden all flat lakes and vowels
folding in on themselves like a rolled tongue.
Pine trees. Reindeer. Stink of damp fur.

Only if I can be Norway.
What, you demand, do you know of Norway?
What is Norway to you? Norway over the sea,
past the flatlands of Hull. Hold me
in the doorway. Hold me in the October twilight.
Be Sweden to my Norway, splitting wood
to my drying fur, bells over a lake,
darkness at midday. Sway me, my Sweden,
under the Northern Lights.

BED 3

My liver is on three percent.
They won't tell me but I know.

I don't need to read the notes
on the end of the bed —

I'm going yellow like pub wallpaper.
Your liver is the Russia of the atlas

of your insides, from the China of your spine
to the Black Sea of your belly.

No Tsar can keep it under his thumb,
no matter how hard he tries.

They look at me — doctors,
junior doctors, faces round the bed

like smudged old masters and they ask me
how I am. You tell me, I say — you're the doctor,

and I wink and they smile like they mean it.
There's an old girl in here had a hip op —

every day she goes past the end of the ward
with a zimmer, getting further and further

by the day. I say that she's Sherpa Tensing
and she laughs. We are passengers on a ship

and she will walk out of here and I won't.

ANDY

He came to the service
but wouldn't stop,
had to get back for the dogs.

Said he only knew her
slightly. But they saw him
once or twice, hanging round

the drive. He never
answered the letters.
Never cashed the cheque.

THE LONGEST DAY

Tina and Tommy are sauntering down West Street,
down West Street through the high noon heat
from happiness to happiness through a world without end.
"Can we cross the street?" Tina asks. "No," says Tommy.
"Oh, can't we," asks Tina, "I want to see our old house,
I want to walk up our old street and see how it is
and see the buddleia." "No," says Tommy again,
"we live on the other side of the estate now."
"Oh just once," says Tina, all nostalgia –
nostalgia is Tina's bestseller, nostalgia
is Tina's buy-one-get-one-free
and she wants to see next door's buddleia,
not knowing that the buy-to-let landlord
cut the buddleia down – the buddleia
that was a fire hydrant, the buddleia
that was an improvised explosive device.
Buy-to-let landlords cannot be expected
to trim buddleias twice a year,
to a buy-to-let landlord a buddleia is dark matter,
a buddleia is the opposite of Return on Investment.
"No, Tina," Tommy says. "We live on the other side
of the estate now." She looks wistfully at the corner shop,
which is the towers and turrets of the past.
"Don't you understand?" Tommy asks,
"we live on the other side of the estate now."

THE PATRON SAINT OF FLOWERS

Some said that the palms of her hands
were brushed with pollen and her voice
could only have been tulip.

Split bulbs drying in the dark
were more their thing – roots waving
their way inside a sack, jumble
of stumps and bald heads.
Not bone grafted to stalk,
how they creak and spit,
marrow and sap.

And what they tied her to
could not have been tree –
greenstick blossomed out of the ash
and made liars of the lot of them,
sticky black tar in two halves
and out of the smoking heap of straw
the yawning throats of lilies.

THE COMMUTER'S GUIDE
TO BRITISH WOODLAND

Walking to work over Woodhouse Ridge,
early Spring and birdsong is covering fire
over my head, wild garlic on my fingers,
a landslide of bluebells falling into the beck.

The man in front of me with the wheelie suitcase
stops to take a photo of the sunlight slanting
at all angles through the branches of a beech,
armfuls and armfuls of water.
He turns to me:

"Crawling like this to our small places,
we're going to be shady all day
under the striplights, coming home
smelling of carpet. Tonight I'll fall asleep
in a Travelodge in the glow
of streetlights under the hum
of swaying traffic. But right now
you and me are crawling
on our hands and knees through landfalls
of daffodils, crying our eyes out
with happiness and hayfever."

I take his arm and we walk together
through the trees, arm in arm
to our respective crawling-places
in Guildford or Leeds,
in Innsbruck or Atascadero, California,
his suitcase scraping along the forest floor,
he to his crawling-place, me to mine,
the birds with brass in their beaks,

a plate-glass sun tipping jugfulls of light over the trees.
We are going to work arm in arm, two grown men
crying our eyes out with happiness and hayfever.

SELF PORTRAIT WITH HUMMINGBIRDS

What is it like to be covered in turquoise
and not even know it? To be nothing more
than a kingfisher flash against silt and treetrunk.

Two hummingbirds are hovering either side
of my head, a drumming in my ears
but drumming is the wrong word.

Does a flower know it's being ransacked?
The bee burrows tighter as if into sunlight itself
until the backs of its legs are panniered,

furry punchdrunk bear with its eyes
streaming, a little drill in a glass jar.
Not the hummingbird, though.

You can't tell where bone ends
and feathers begin, any more
than you can say with certainty

where the colour came from.
In this case, delicate has come
from delicate, petal from feather,

beak from stamen, and a colour
you only get underground
has card-tricked out of thin air.

TOWPATH

Something is singing
down by the canal – very human,
like foxes or a bird in a fox's mouth.
Only the few who ever heard it ever guessed
that something so heavy in the water
could sing like this – rust-white,
cork and eiderdown, more snake than cygnet.

The swan – soapstone,
feathered jet – is on its own
and it mates for life,
it's going to die
and this is one last dusk.
But that's not why it's crying
above the crash of the weir.

THE CARETAKER COMPARES HIMSELF
TO THE HAPPIEST MAN ALIVE

Freddie Mercury employed a butler
to serve cocaine on a silver salver.
Me, however – I've been a caretaker
for thirty years, give or take –

I had a spell
as Creative Director
of the Royal Opera House,
Covent Garden –

but now I've got to get up at half six
and work one Saturday in four, locking doors,
unlocking doors, switching off lights, moving chairs
for layabout provincial thespians.
"But you get free tickets," they say down the pub –
not seeing that I got free tickets at Covent Garden
but would give them away to incredulous
Community Support Officers,
who doubtless sold them on eBay.

Anyway,
the Happiest Man Alive
does not have to get up at half six
or work one Saturday in four
and does not have to put up
with the square outside full of ladyboys.

How I wish I was caretaker for the ladyboys,
the ladyboys who come every year from Bangkok –
all the way from Bangkok and I would come with them
and move not chairs and water-coolers

but armfuls and armfuls of sequin bodices,
piles of lilies, stargazer lilies making me sneeze
and lashing my new tan with sticky bitter welts –
on my arms, my shoulders, the teeshirt I bought in Dortmund
so that when I go on my break and stand in the rain
smoking a fag people look at me strangely
covered in suntan and pollen and I smile and say
"Yes! I am caretaker to the ladyboys
of Bangkok! And I'm on my fag break!
The Happiest Man Alive!"

WHAT HAPPENS NEXT IS AMAZING

My great granddad climbs out of the wet earth,
claws his way past tree roots and the ashes of his sisters,
he splits out of the ground and he's new like broken china.
"Too much leaning back in the dark," he says stretching
in the sunshine and he squints at me while his eyes adjust.

It's true what they say – your hair grows underground,
you grow out of your graveclothes like school uniform.
He wants to know what we've been up to,
if the house is the same, what happened to the kids.
Never mind flowers he could murder a fag.

By the time I can speak he's striding off towards the bus stop
and the sun's gone in. I want to ask him what it's like.
"It's like being alive!" he shouts without looking round.
"Being dead's like being alive!"

LAZARUS AWAKE

My name is Lazarus. I used to work
for United Dairies — not, you understand,
as a milkman. I was an office-creeper,
I crept around the office sorting invoices,
delivery notes, dunning people for payment.
Only occasionally did I hear the rattle
of milk bottles in their crates, and even then
it was far off, notional — there they go, I'd say,
and think of the milk rattling off
to its early-morning doorsteps, in the days
when milkmen left milk on people's doorsteps.

Then one day I dropped down dead.
That's what people said — dropped down dead.
It was a Bank Holiday, I had gone to move the car,
I was a long time moving the car
and Sandra looked out the kitchen window
and saw my feet lying in the drive, sticking out
from behind the car, and she ran out
and I had dropped down dead.

So far, so inevitable. Hundreds of people
drop down dead every day
and I happened to be one of them.
I am assured that Sandra was devastated,
there was a big turnout for the funeral,
it was a good send-off, it cost a fortune.
(I was cross with Sandra about that,
I always said I didn't want any fuss —
just chuck me over the back fence, I'd joke —
play John Coltrane and chuck me over the back fence.)

I must say Sandra's tougher than I thought.
It's no easy thing for the husband you've just,
or so you thought, said goodbye to at the Crem
turn up on your doorstep after the wake
when everyone's gone except Pauline
who's washing up and making herself useful.
(Pauline has been a brick.) I didn't know what to do –
I was fairly stunned myself – three days,
four days dead, nearly a week and suddenly,
before I know where I am, I'm walking
into the early June sunshine, a lovely Spring day,
making my way home along the inner ringroad
in my best suit, the suit we bought for my niece's wedding.

She took it surprisingly well – said,
after she'd stopped crying, that it was just like me,
entirely like me, whatever that's supposed to mean.
I don't know what I'm going to do now.
Sandra says I can sleep in the spare room,
she says she needs time to think,
but I don't think I can stay. I may only have been dead
for a few days – I'm not really sure how long,
can you ever tell how long you've been asleep
without looking at the clock? – but people move on
very quickly, or Sandra does: she's already
given my clothes to the PDSA.
And there's the paperwork. My life insurance
will pay out any day, a tidy sum, enough to live on
if I can take myself away, away to the East Coast,
rent a cottage in Filey or Flamborough or near Spurn Point,
I want to sit with Spurn Point on the tip of my tongue
under the cry of gulls with the lighthouse hauling its huge light
into the sea and work out the meaning of it –
dead in the drive, alive at Spurn Point,

grief like a lost limb, phantom pains,
a weight that isn't there, the lighthouse in the night,
the cry of gulls, the meaning of it.

A FLY IN LATE DECEMBER

You can't even remember
when there were seasons –
when flies like me
were long dead by late December,
legs folded in like deckchairs.
But here I am living it up
in a pop-up bar in the foothills
of Bradford, sharp as anything,
a bluebottle in my dotage.
You have no idea of the chandelier turning
of my eyes, the cut glass on the ends
of my legs, the endless inviting adventure
of the moonscape dustfields
above your heads. I am a craft
landing four-square
without a sound, without coming up for air.
If I was as big as you
my wings would be creaking film
sliding open in the dark.

HIVE

Do you remember the cat
that hung from my arm like a glove –
blood under the tap and I promised not to cry?
The beekeeper dipping his hands into all that fury.

Sometimes I see you open your mouth
and nothing comes out except bees,
your eyes swaying with them,
the palms of your hands a swarm.

I'm not much more than the blue birds
that landed on me, the bones in my ears
were feathers and all I could hear
was them chirping *Here he is! Here he is! Here!*

SECOND DEATH

If it's true that after seven years
every cell in the body has renewed itself
then you only really died in 2003
only this time I hardly noticed,
I was my own dawn chorus of cells refreshing
as the sky above Baghdad lit up,
I was plush and colourful and I was alive
in the same way you were arrows
falling to earth or a tide coming in,
triumph and triumph and triumph
over the gravemouth all of us
are up to our knees in. So what
if my hands are two casts
and my hair is mitochondria?
So what if my face is part deathmask
and when I speak my voice
is almost your voice?